AF143910

1

WISDOM
OF THE
WARRIOR OF LIGHT

WISDOM

OF THE

WARRIOR OF LIGHT

Guy-Noël AUBRY

Édition : BoD – Books on Demand
12/14 rond-point des Champs-Élysées, 75008 Paris
Impression : BoD - Books on Demand, Norderstedt,
Allemagne
ISBN : 9782322238330
Dépôt légal : Novembre 2020

This book is dedicated to all the brave men and women who walk this earth with a deep desire to be true to themselves and the world, to do good, and to be at peace with themselves.

The struggle begins within oneself...

Before - About

This book is a homage to Paulo Coelho's book Manuel of the Warrior of Light. I read this book when I was young and I really appreciated the greatness of soul that emanated from the Warrior.

Life experiences, long meditations and study led me to find my own path and to have a vision sometimes different from the one I had as a young man. And while on the whole I agree with what the Warrior said, I believe that another light of wisdom shining in this world will be welcome.

Another pearl found in the ocean of our hearts, exposed to the sight of men (who seek wisdom) and poured into the treasury of humanity's wisdom is a good thing.

Thus, another Warrior of Light is not too many in this world and many more are needed.

Most of the stories in this inspiring, funny or intriguing book are unpublished. Some, however, although known to a few, have been reprinted for their beauty and richness.

In a first reading, it may appear to the reader a certain form of disorder. This disorder is the image of a life of adventure when one is a Warrior of Light.

The reader should therefore not bother looking for a particular order in these stories. There is no link between them except the first, the last and the penultimate.

In my fraternal intention, I have conceived this collection of stories and present it, like a friend who offers another a box of sweets whose bottom he cannot see and asks him to dip his hand into it, confiding in him at random. When he puts his hand in, he sometimes picks up a chocolate, sometimes a candy, or a nougat or something else...

Finally, this book is metaphorical The power of a book depends more on who reads it than who writes it.

The wise man may derive his substance from few things, while the ignorant in the face of abundance may remain hungry.

In order for a book to instruct, improve, and penetrate a reader, the reader must have some mastery of the material it contains, or at least the desire to master it.

The sword of the Warrior, for example, represents his greatest talent. For one it will be to teach, for the other to heal or take care of others, another still will have the easy joy that he will be able to give in sharing ...

The shield is its ability to withstand the blows, its resilience. The shoes of the Warrior are his seat on the ground and thus his principles of life, the values he believes in and fights for. It can be family, love, justice, God, peace, wisdom... The fights he fights are not all physical, they can be emotional or spiritual.

From all of the above, the reader can deduce that it is not enough to read this book at the first level to benefit from it, but that he will benefit more by reading it at three levels.

The descriptive level, the metaphorical level, and the implicit level (i.e., how to implement this idea or concept in my life).

The most beneficial for the reader are the bridges he or she will build between what he or she reads and his or her concrete life.

The ultimate goal of knowledge is not to be accumulated, but to be liberated and used to bring about an evolution, a transformation; this is the ultimate goal of co-naissance.

Additional note:

If, at the beginning, I had in mind a book for adults, several people who participated in its enrichment and correction found that it would also be very interesting for teenagers, and even for children.

It would only be necessary for parents to accompany the younger ones and help them understand the moral of each story. They would then be able to draw a lesson from it for the situations they will face in their daily life (family and school).

With teenagers, in particular, this book can be a support for discussions between parents and teenagers. It would then serve as an interface from which to exchange about problem situations, which would otherwise be more difficult to initiate.

I hadn't thought of that, but I think it's a great idea. I am therefore pleased to dedicate this book also to children and young people who wish to be like the Warrior of Light, whether they are boys or girls; for bravery, greatness of spirit and intelligence are not the prerogative of one or the other, but belong to both.

I also dedicate this book to children, young people, and to those who wish to be like the Warrior of Light.

Good and beautiful readings, beautiful meditations and beautiful discussions ...

See you soon,

Guy-Noël AUBRY

Introduction

The greatest book of Wisdom in the world is open before the eyes of every man. It was written by the greatest of all sages, God.

Men, trees, animals, and the countless situations it contains are so many sentences and paragraphs assembled before him. He who has not exercised his intelligence sufficiently does not understand these things. He does not understand that everything is there exposed before his eyes and that the situations that unfold there are so many lessons of wisdom.

Few begin to understand this book, and even fewer persevere in their study, for almost all of them are busy. They run after time, they run after money, they run after honors, they run endlessly ... not understanding that their race is lost in advance ... So they spend their whole lives running until their strength leaves them ...

Those who are truly powerful are masters of their time.

Conversely, he who has exercised his heart to free himself from worries and fears has become master of himself. He crosses this Earth as one crosses a garden. Admirable garden that this one. The innocent and candid eye perceives it in its purity. He hears a marvelous melody that only an attentive ear perceives and understands. With his liberated mind, he embraces the immensity of the world and its diversity. He enters in harmony with the world and nature. He understands the river that sings as well as the one that cries without saying a word. He understands the Work as a whole, he is at peace.

And while he rests in peace, his soul at peace, a melody reaches his ears; a voice whispers to him: show the way to your brothers...

be

wise as snakes

and

innocent

as doves

(S. Mattew 10,16)

1) The Fight with the Master or the need to face one's fears

- Come at once, orders the Master. Take your sword and your combat equipment.

A master has trained the Warrior. For three long years, he taught him all his blows. Here he proposes to the Warrior of Light one last fight, a fight to the death!
The Warrior remembers how strong he thought he was on his first day and how the master could have killed him 100 times when they first met.

- I refuse, said the Warrior, *you risk killing me.*
- The man you used to be is no more! And the man you will be is not yet... He will never be if you don't face your fears.

The warrior reflects and thinks that the master could have easily killed him in his sleep the night before if that was his intention.

The battle begins tense, uncertain. The blows multiply. They rain quickly and surprisingly. With a leap, as sharp as that of the

Cobra, the master is on his left, the warrior parries the attack in extremis. With a rotation, he is now on his right, the warrior with a quick slide, comes out of the axis of striking, seizes this brief break in the opponent's movement, takes advantage of the tiny opening of the opponent's guard and wounds him in the hand, the sword falls.

The one who previously taught him everything about the art of combat is now at his mercy. Finally, the Warrior believes it!

Surprise! The master takes out of his pectoral a shorter sword, more adapted to close combat.

Now it is up to the warrior to be in trouble. He did not expect such a resource. Here he is encumbered by his sword which has become too long. He retreats, his opponent pursues him, his blade just misses his left cheek, then his right cheek.

The Warrior is unable to place his sword between him and the assailant for such a short distance. He knows that his master is right-handed and that he is less skillful and less strong with his left hand, the one holding the small blade, yet he seems just as skillful as before. The warrior understands, it is the energy of despair.

Without thinking, he hits the master's foot hard with the point of the sword. This unexpected tactic surprises the master who is much slower in his movements. The warrior springs to one side and stings the other foot, the master collapses, wounded.

- *You've won!,* says the one who was once stronger than him. *Choose life and spare me. Allow me to teach where you will not be!*

- *Here is your domain*, replied the new Master. I will go elsewhere.

And he left.[1]

---

[1] This story is commented and explained in detail in the second part of the book.

2) **The fire lit by the children** or how to carry out any project with enthusiasm, measure and perseverance.

The Warrior of Light observes the children lighting a fire. They are all joyful about their powers: some put twigs, others sheets of paper, some add stones around it, another throws a flammable cube and the fire is ready.

They join together to throw the burning matches. That's it, the fire has started, the first sparks come out, then the first flames. Here they are making rounds and antics around the fire; they get dizzy.

Carried away by their joy, some of them load the nascent fire with heavy logs, and the little fire that had just been born goes out and dies.

The Warrior understands that many things are necessary to start a fire.

It sometimes takes a lot of time and energy to set up projects, habits, relationships...

Many things work this way...

And as soon as you start, you want to do too much, then everything collapses, goes out and dies. We find ourselves in sadness, disappointment and failure ...

It is better to make the fire grow first... [2]

---

[2] The subtitle of the story takes its full meaning when reading the explanations in the second part of the book.

3) Strength of conviction and beauty

The Warrior of Light is walking near a beautiful forest. It is small, but so beautiful! And today there is a great agitation, everything is upset... An army of diggers, bulldozers and lumberjacks decimate the trees methodically without any pity. They don't want to leave a single one!

- *What are you doing!* throws the Warrior to the one who seems to be the leader of these operations.
- *We have orders to cut down all trees without exception. A subdivision should soon emerge here.*

And now the chainsaws are starting up again. They cross the heart of the softwoods. The stronger ones are laid down by the armada of bulls.

Some, however, resist valiantly, they have deep roots and cling with conviction. They smoke, squeak, but the trees hold on.

The Warrior understands that it is the same for the men. It is the strength of their convictions that enables them to hold on in the face of adversity.

Work is stopped to assess the situation. The promoter is called. Here he comes. He notes the progress of the work.

- Why are some trees still standing?

The foreman explains to him that there is a high risk of breakage. The developer orders that the layout of the houses be changed to avoid financial losses.

- And this one says the developer, pointing his finger at it, *he doesn't look as strong as the others.*
- Come, the person in charge answers, *come and see for yourself.*

Approaching, the promoter notices that he is covered with myriads and myriads of tiny, magnificent flowers that scent the air with an indefinable fragrance, and he contemplates the birds that sing delicately under his branches, as if bewitched by their scent.

- Leave it too, concludes the promoter looks dreamy, *place my daughter's house in front of him, so I can continue to admire it when I come to see it.*

The Warrior understands that beauty is also a strength...

4) To be or to appear?

The Warrior of Light does not try to appear more than he is, nor less. He knows that this is not what will make him better.

He doesn't try to appear, he tries to be, and that absorbs all his energy. His friends tell him: *Put on your best face!*

He doesn't listen to them, he doesn't follow them. Then they move away from him, because he is not bright and sparkling enough in their eyes.

The Warrior knows that well cut zirconia can appear to many as a beautiful diamond, but not to the expert.

That is why the Warrior remains true to himself. He prefers to be loved by a few for what he truly is, rather than by many for what he is not!

5) The Cat and the chicks or how to choose the right strategy

The blackbird's nest fell from the low branch of an orange tree. Here are the two small birds on the ground, barely recovering from their fall. The louder of the two is calling out; he is hoping for his mother.

The other, dizzy from its fall and scared, runs to take refuge in the tall grass near the tree trunk.

The cat, alerted by all this agitation, arrives before anyone else. With soft footsteps, he approaches and notices the windfall. It takes out its claws, and with a leap, here it is on the one that was previously self-sabotaging. He swallows it all of a sudden without any further ado.

The second, motionless, holds his breath. The cat looks for a moment, turns and returns smelling like another prey, but he doesn't find it and leaves.

The Warrior learns a lesson. Sometimes, the best fighting strategy is not to call for reinforcements, but to be invisible to the enemy...

6) Sometimes you have to keep your secrets

The Warrior of Light teaches what he knows to others. Voices whisper to him: keep these secrets to yourself, you will benefit from them.

Others tell him: choose carefully who you are around and who you open your heart to.

The Warrior remembers that Jesus did not tell everyone everything, but revealed his greatest secrets to his intimate Peter, James and John.

So the Warrior listens to the voice of wisdom, he does not spread his knowledge.

That is why when he is asked a question, sometimes he answers and other times he does not. He keeps silent and smiles.

And when one insists, he simply says: The time has not yet come...

7) Choose the right opponents

The Warrior of Light knows that in order to win many battles, one must carefully choose one's learning and training partners.

An opponent who is too weak will not make him progress. An opponent who is too strong could hurt or discourage him.

That is why the Warrior prefers to choose opponents who are within his reach, but a little stronger than him. Thus, he fights to the best of his possibilities; and he progresses.

Sometimes the Warrior loses, but for a defeat, he counts two or three victories.

- *As he often loses!* say those who spy on him.

But the Warrior knows that this is the right ratio, the one that allows him to progress the fastest and that will save him when the combat will be for good.

8) Intimacy leads to simplicity

The Warrior of Light knows that everything is complicated before being simple. It takes about a year for a baby to pronounce its first words and two years for a simple sentence. Now that he's older, it's a game to him.

So if a situation seems confusing or complicated to the Warrior, it's because he hasn't spent enough time with her yet, so she still resists his analysis or intuition.

To know her well, he discusses with her, as one discusses with a friend and observes her from several angles, as one observes a work of art. When they get to know each other better, everything will be simple.

This is how Archimedes proceeded. He took his problem with him everywhere: how to know if the king's crown is made of pure gold without touching its integrity?

It seemed impossible, yet Archimedes solved the problem by taking his problem with him in his bath.

9) The Queen in chess or it is necessary to know your main weapon in life.

The Warrior of Light sits in the shade of a tree in a large park. In the distance children play ball, closer a father teaches his son chess.

The Warrior pays attention to what he says:

- The Queen is the most powerful piece in the game. She is your greatest asset. So sooner or later the enemy will try to attack her.

- If you lose her, you will be in great difficulty. Protect her well and I will teach you how.

The Warrior thinks and wonders what his main weapon is...

He now knows what he must protect and defend.

10) Love and handling of the sword

The Warrior of Light has a heart to live and to love.

He never goes out without having inflated it with kind thoughts, this is his love training. This exercise precedes the sword and bow exercises.

The Warrior has noticed that his effectiveness in handling weapons is intimately linked to his level of love.

The more he is in love, the more he becomes one with his sword.

And the same goes for his bow. The more non-judgmental he is, the more precisely he directs his arrow.

The stiffness of the heart is linked to the stiffness of the body.

11) The flower - the bee and the star
or why you shouldn't pick a flower unnecessarily

The Warrior of Light is walking around in the forest. At the bend of a clearing, he sees a family that seems happy. His heart rejoices in this apparent harmony.

The little boy is having fun pushing his balloon down the slope that keeps coming back to him, he enjoys it. Sometimes he misses it and his father behind him sends it back to him.

The older little girl shows a pretty flower to her mother.

- Mommy, look how pretty it is! I'm going to pick it for you.

And the little girl, happy to please her beloved mommy, picks it up and puts it in her hair. Here they are all happy and laughing.

The afternoon passes and on the way back the Warrior finds the family still there who is about to leave.

- Come, says the father to his son!

But the son does not listen to him. He remembers the flower that his sister picked for his mother and he too wants to take one, but a much bigger one.

- *Come, my darling*, insists the mother. Leave the flower, it's there with her friends.

The Father takes a harder line, *leave the flower and come and help us*.

But the little boy can't hear anything. He pulls with all his strength and patatras! A piece of the stump on which the flower had grown goes with it. And here the hive that had found refuge in the dead tree is discovered.

The bees rush on the assailant. It is panic. The father runs towards the crying son who does not know what to do and carries him away with a volley of stings.

He who needlessly picks a flower disturbs a star; he breaks the harmony of life.

The bee watches over the star!

Life gives us signs and warnings, but not everyone understands them, so they go crescendo. Sometimes it is only when we sting ourselves that we understand that it is better to listen.

12) Problems are opportunities for growth

The Warrior of Light knows that many peoples have wandered and lost their way for lack of knowledge. That is why every day he seeks to learn an eternal truth and a temporal truth.

An intelligence has been given to him and like a sword, it must be sharpened every day on the great millstone of life that turns without stopping.

The problems that arise before him today are opportunities for growth; they are his teachers of the day.

They are ordained for his progress and proportionate to his growth.

They are there for his learning and developing his intelligence.

Far from regimented against them, he blesses them as a gift that life gives him to grow.

13) Seed and Harvest - An Invitation to Patience

The Warrior of Light knows that there is a time lag between the throwing of the seed and the harvest.

It is not by stamping against the night that the day arrives faster.

The seed that explodes under the ground does not reveal the young shoot until a few days after this decisive event.

Sometimes the results seem to be slow in coming, but just because you can't see anything doesn't mean that nothing is happening. This is the law of nature and it applies to everyone.

Effort is a virtue, patience also.

14) Prepare a lamp when it's daylight - Invitation to action.

Whoever wants to go fishing must prepare his nets.

Whoever wants to hunt must check his bow and arrow.

If one wants light throughout the night, one must prepare a sufficient reserve of oil and a lamp while the day is still there. After that it will be too late!

Patience is a virtue, so is effort.

15) The labyrinth

The Warrior of Light knows the importance of time, because he knows that it is not eternal. It is the rarity of something that makes it his price. He often asks himself if he uses it well.

Are his actions true, beautiful and good; faithful to his values? Are they useful?

While the Warrior wonders, a little boy comes to him with his play book.

- *John, leave the man in peace*, his mother tells him, somewhat worried.

But the little boy does not listen to her. He looks at the Warrior with his innocent eye.

- *I can't do it*, he tells him, pointing to a maze starting at several points and leading to several doors, all closed except one.

He ingeniously questions the Warrior:
- *Which starting point should I choose to fall on the only open door?*

- *It is very simple*, answers him this one. *It is enough to start the labyrinth upside down. Start from the open door and go back up the thread, you will find the right starting point.*

The child happily runs back to his mother. She smiles at the Warrior, looking a little embarrassed that her son has disturbed a stranger. He shouts out his joy:
- Mommy, mommy, I know how to do it, I know how to do it.

The Warrior leaves them to their joy and resumes his reflections: are my actions good, are they useful? ...

Suddenly, it is enlightenment! He understands. Sometimes by solving other people's problems, we find answers to our own. By solving Little John's problem, the Warrior had solved his own!

We have to take the problem backwards, like in the labyrinth: Who do I want to become? Who do I want to be in the end? And that way, he will know the way.

The Warrior then decides to order his actions to whoever he is in power and everything becomes clearer...
The Warrior is guided.

16) The warrior and the battle of hearts

When the Warrior of Light talks to someone who doesn't want to listen, he doesn't pass in force. He is silent.

- *As he is easily confused*, whispers those who observe him.

- *How weak he is*, add the others.

The warrior is neither weak nor confused. He is based on the rock. His convictions are unshakeable.

Just as the river that winds its way to the sea and sometimes takes a detour to get there, he accepts to "lose" the battle of words to win the war of hearts.

17) The warrior is just in charge of sowing

The Warrior of Light knows that if he has a responsibility in this world, so do others.

So if sometimes he is in charge of sowing, growing or harvesting, he also knows that more often than not, he is only in charge of sowing, showing or lighting.

He must detach himself from the result; it does not belong to him, but is the fruit of the other's freedom; it is the latter alone who will decide (or not) to water the seed and make it germinate.

18) Take a deep breath

The Warrior of Light often stops to consider with a child's eye the wonders that surround him and to which sometimes he had not paid attention.

He takes the opportunity to take a deep breath and these two things do him a lot of good.

19) The warrior seeks to defeat himself

The Warrior of Light knows that he will have to fight every day for truth and love.

He also knows that the most important and decisive battle is within himself.

So rather than seeking to defeat others, he seeks instead to defeat himself, to love himself and to love others.

20) The warrior at the airplane counter or true wealth

The Warrior of Light is at the boarding counter. He walks towards the hostess and is about to hand her his ticket and here is a well-dressed man shoving him without care:

- *Get out of the way, I'm an important man!*
- *For who?* Answer simply the Warrior.

The man is somewhat bewildered by this question. After a brief moment, he ends up answering: *For everyone, I own many companies and tens of millions, get out of my way!*

Since when is wealth a mark of nobility!

However, the Warrior is calm and curious, he moves aside and listens to what happens next.

- *I need a ticket immediately in first class*, he says bluntly to the hostess.

- *Sorry sir*, she answers politely, *our first class is full, we can offer you a ticket in intermediate class for 1000 €.*

- *You're crazy, that's the price of first class! I still prefer to travel in economy class!*

And here is the "rich" man pulling out his credit card while grumbling and moaning, preferring to travel in economy class when he could be more comfortable in intermediate class!

The Warrior smiles within himself: the man thought he was rich, but in his heart, he was still poor!

This one is really rich who is not attached to any good; nothing costs him, nothing is too expensive.

21) Every divided kingdom collapses

The Warrior of Light knows from Christ's teaching that every divided kingdom collapses. He has seen for himself the unfortunate truth of this word.

How many families, how many powers, how many kingdoms of the earth have collapsed as a result of infighting and division!

That is why the Warrior of Light is neither divided within himself nor divided. He knows that this division is a fragility which, if it is not resorbed, will eventually lead him to total ruin; it will not happen in a day, but it will happen.

So the warrior first seeks unity within himself. His external words and actions are the pure and sincere manifestations of who he is internally. Seeing one of them gives a glimpse of his soul.

22) The Warrior seeks the meaning of his life in signs, the date of his baptism and other things ...

The Warrior of Light knows that the most important questions of his life revolve around his being. Who are you? What is your destiny? Who do you want to be?

He seeks the answers in the values he believes in, in the actions that make him happy or sad. And he finds a first layer of answers.

Then the warrior digs deeper. He wants to find valuable and buried information. He makes a reading of the great events of his life and draws up a summary by decade. He wants to be able to summarize his life in a paragraph of a few lines or better yet condense it into a single line!

- *What is he is looking for with so much energy*, are asking his friends, with a curiosity mixed with anxiety.

He is still searching in ways that seem to others to be pure madness or fantasy: the conditions of his conception - Which saint presided over his birth? - Why did he receive this name? - What is the saint of his baptism? - What was important to him as a child? What were his dreams then?

- *How original and eccentric he is!* Say those who see him searching.

The Warrior wants to understand who he is and the meaning of his life, because what men call chance, wise men call coincidence and others call destiny. He knows that he is part of the great tapestry of humanity. Some threads are directly connected to each other from behind; if one pulls on one, the other comes.

The observer of this world does not know it, because he does not see that, but the one who conceived the canvas knows it. It is for having received this vision that the Warrior of Light knows that all this data: his name, the day of his birth, the saint who presides over his birth, the one who presides over his baptism... All this has a meaning that is connected to his life.

He synthesizes his observations and hypotheses, which are all questions thrown to the universe. And he knows that the universe will answer him, as it has already begun to do, because Christ said :

"He who seeks finds
and to whomever asks, it will be given".

23) The Warrior of Light and Patience - He who is proud gets impatient with everything

The Warrior of Light knows that he who is proud is impatient with everything, while he who is perfectly humble is without pride; he offers no hold to the world.

Patience is a manifestation of humility and love.

The warrior never loses an opportunity to practice both.

24) The Warrior cultivates his forces as one cultivates his garden.

The Warrior of Light cultivates his forces as one cultivates his garden. He observes what makes his joy and peace grow, and drinks from it regularly.

He has already tasted many springs and it has become clear to him that they are not all as healthy and good as each other.

His fellow students go to many springs and seem to enjoy them. They question the warrior:
- *Why don't you come with us to taste this new spring or this new cup of drunkenness?*

- *There is too much danger in following you*, he reply.

The warrior knows that if you dip your lips in too many cups, you always end up poisoning yourself.

The warrior of light always chooses his sources carefully, that's why he is always in the camp of life.

25) The Warrior sometimes gets angry

The Warrior of Light sometimes gets into holy anger. He does not fear it, nor that of others.

Christ Himself sometimes became angry: when He drove the vendors out of the Temple, when He saw the lack of faith of His disciples on the return from His Transfiguration, when He saw the hardening of heart of His compatriots who did not want to heal a paralyzed man on a Sabbath.

His anger was an expression of his Justice and Holiness; the consequence of the injustices he saw in the world.

The same is true for the warrior. His anger lasted only a moment. He knows that it is an effective but dangerous weapon. She is like a burning rag that one holds.

It may be useful for a while, but it must not be maintained for too long, otherwise you get burned.

It is still like the fire on a branch taken from the hearth of Holy Justice and held to illuminate injustice, to make it recede like a wild animal.

But one cannot keep this flame eternally, otherwise the fire rises up to the hand and then to the whole being; it is then that one is consumed!

26) The disciple and the elephant

A disciple comes to see the Warrior and asks him:

- *Can you teach me how to fight?*
- *First I must show you something. Come with me.*

The master takes his new disciple to the circus. He is intrigued by the destination.

The Warrior of Light, like many who teach wisdom, does not take the path most frequented by spectators and followers. So they both arrive behind the big top.

- *Observe this elephant*, said the Warrior. *Look at its imposing size and build, its imposing muscles. How is it that he does not go away?*

The disciple gazed for a moment at the imposing padlock and the sturdy chain that held the elephant in place.

He was about to answer when he noticed something strange: the stake that held it together was simply fixed in the ground, without any particular seal.

- *I don't know*, answered the somewhat perplexed disciple. *Perhaps he thinks he cannot free himself, because he considers the padlock and the chain. But if he looked at his strength and saw what the chain was attached to, he would understand that everything that holds him back is just an illusion.*

- *You have spoken well*, the Warrior tells him; *did you figure out what I pointed out to you?*

And with these words he left him to his meditations.

27) Fear is necessary or how the warrior considers fear

The Warrior of Light must fight today in a very famous tournament. He is the big favorite and everyone has their eye on his deeds; his reputation preceded him. It is said of him that he can know an opponent's weak point at a glance and defeat him even before he has drawn his sword.

- It seems that he still has a slight apprehension before engaging the fight, despite all his victories, astonish those who attend the tournament.

The Warrior of Light does not listen to them. He is more wary of pride than of fear. His victories have given him confidence, and fear has moved away from him. This fear was necessary for his training, it taught him to strengthen himself and to remain vigilant.

He used fear like a dumbbell, but he knows that pride will lead him to his downfall if he doesn't repress it. For pride only gives him illusory assurance. This is why the warrior prefers a hint of fear to a hint of pride.

28) The Warrior heals his body and soul

The Warrior of Light did not know only victories. He has also had his share of defeats, and it is not those he has received by the sword that have done him the most harm.

His soul has also been wounded a few times, and the wound was all the more painful when the blow was struck by someone close or trusted.

Therefore, the Warrior does not only heal his body, but also his soul. He massages his body with oil, olive or arnica oil and he massages his soul with the oil of prayer and forgiveness.

29) Letting go of the past for ...

The master who trained him in the past had taken away his sword more than once, to give him a better one.

And although it was objectively better, he often regretted his old sword before he fully appreciated the new one.

The same is true of life! This is why the Warrior lets go of the past to better grasp the present and thus be ready to welcome the blessings of the future.

30) The Disciple and the reflection on the lake

A young man comes to see the Warrior in the middle of the night.

- *I would like to be as wise as you*, said the young man.

- *Who said I was wise?* replied the Warrior.

- *In the village many say it and others retort that you are mad.*

- *Because some say I am mad, then perhaps I am wise, for wisdom seems madness to those who are stuck in the world.*

- *I see that you are a Master of thought. How long will it take me to acquire Wisdom from you?*

- *That depends on you. Some of the best disciples took two years, some five, some ten, and some went before that.*

- *If I work twice as hard as the best of them will I take a year instead of two?*

- Come and see the lake with me. See how it reflects the sky, the stars and the moon. Now throw a stone and tell me what you see.

The young man does it. He now sees only the moon, and still with difficulty. He only has a distorted image of it. He recognizes it more by its clarity than by its characteristic shape.

How could the sky be reflected on a turbulent lake!

- You see, said the Warrior, *a restless spirit shaken with precipitation can no longer reflect the sky. This spirit reflects only the crudest truths of existence. Precipitation, inner tensions, lusts slow down or prevent your spiritual progress.*

Wisdom is established only in a calm spirit. Wisdom is a reflection of heaven. [3]

---

[3] This story is commented in the second part

31) Like the flower that turns into fruit, the warrior is transformed.

The Warrior of Light had set himself the goal of having a beautiful garden. He has been cultivating it regularly for three years now.

He has been working on this task in parallel with his training and travels. He now has a beautiful garden full of vegetables, flowers and fruit trees.

The Warrior of Light is savoring his success. He has worked hard for it. He takes a basket and goes to collect what belongs to him, brings it back to his house and starts to sort it out.

While he separates the fruit from the vegetables, birds start to sing. This is not the usual song of contentment or a love parade. He recognizes the warning cries of danger. The warrior has become more attentive.

He looks out the window and sees four men on their mounts a hundred meters away.

They were certainly thinking of taking some fruit discreetly from the warrior, but now that they are discovered, they prefer to leave.

The warrior is happy, he goes back to his fruits and vegetables, compares their color, shape, texture and smell. He is in harmony with life.

While he is doing this, a thought comes into his mind: not only does he have more through this garden project, but something almost mysterious has happened in addition.

As he worked on his work, he improved little by little. His body became stronger and more supple. He has become more patient and enduring. His mind became more attentive and alert.

The warrior understands that the most important thing in the adventure is not only the result, but also the new person he becomes as the project unfolds.

32) Brick, wall and cathedral

The Warrior of Light sees three men in his dream working. Something intrigues him: they are both the same and different.

He calls the first one and says:
- *What are you doing?*
- *I'm laying a brick as well as I can and I don't worry about the rest, the rest will come by itself.*

And when he gives his answer, he goes back to his work.

The Warrior calls the second who seems to be doing the same thing, but whose gaze appears different. He asks him the same question:
- *What are you doing here?*
- *I am building a wall; to do so, I check the alignment of the bricks between them.*

And his answer given, he goes back to his work.

The Warrior calls the third, and asks him one last time:

- What is your work?

- I am building a cathedral; for that I check the arrangement of the walls in relation to each other.

And the Warrior understands that this dream is a metaphor for his life.

Living in the present moment is important to lay the brick of each day properly, but you have to check that you have pressed it against the right wall.

Some people walk correctly, but they are not heading in the right direction.

The warrior also understands that if the walls are scattered, the construction will never be finished, so you also need a global vision.

The brick, the wall and the cathedral, all three are necessary. The warrior wakes up and carefully notes this lesson given to him by the angels.

33) The ambush or knowing what you are capable of

The Warrior of Light rides on his steed. He goes to the clearing where a duel awaits him. When he arrives, he sees his opponent assisted by ten others!

The Warrior spins and turns back immediately and goes away with his bridle down.

- *Since he is a coward*, the eleven men who were waiting for him with firm feet throw them out.

Who is the coward, who is the deceiver? The one who comes to fight faithfully or the one who comes with ten others who will fight at his side?

The Warrior knows what he is capable of and above all what he is not capable of; it is a great grace! His blood would have been shed in this clearing mixed with that of six or seven other Warriors. He would not have come out alive from this unfair and unequal fight.

This world lacks neither bloodshed nor death. If he withdraws, it is to honor the life entrusted to him. This world does not need one more corpse, it needs more light.

The Warrior knows that he has made the right decision. All those who have gone before him in this kind of ambush testify to this, whether they are alive or dead. Those who have died have more often been victims of their lack of judgment than of surprise.

They fell into fear of the gaze of others before falling under the gaze of swords.

The warrior has too often seen his friends fall under both to know it. He has other battles to fight.

34) Blows must be unpredictable or cunning in the service of life.

The Warrior of Light observes how other warriors fight, whether they are of light or darkness.

He notices that the most effective blows lose their effectiveness when they are predictable. He infers that the surprise and unpredictability of the blows are superior to a blow considered more effective, but anticipated by the opponent.

Then the Warrior turns over against the observer what he learned from him. He feigns, he pretends to strike a blow in one way, but finally strikes it in another... and often the advantage proves decisive and the wounded opponent abandons the fight.

- *How cunning he is!* some say
- *He is cheating!* retort the others.

There is no rule in a fight to the death, except that of winning and listening to one's conscience.

The warrior is happy to have spared a life thanks to his cunning, his own or that of the opponent.

35) The warrior looks behind him to better advance

The Warrior of Light goes to visit his mother. The one who fed him with her breasts and rocked him on his hips. She has a special place in the warrior's heart. When he looks at her, his child's soul resurfaces more easily.

He arrives in sight of the house and sees her climbing the attic stairs that cover the whole house. She has undertaken to tidy up the vast attic. The warrior approaches his mother and kisses her.

She says to him: *There are too many objects that accumulate here and decay. We won't use them anymore. Let's give them away so that they can experience another life. They will bring other laughter and other moments of happiness.*

The mother of the warrior is generous and full of good sense. The warrior knows that life is movement. It is necessary that objects circulate like the water of the rivers. From this water that runs over the rocks and swirls in a joyful whirl, he can drink; but if it stagnates, it loses its dynamism. It then degrades little by little and becomes corrupt. The water must keep its movement to keep its life force. This is how it will bring vigor and joy.

It is the same for objects. If they are piled up out of sight, they will one day be forgotten. There, away from everyone, they no longer fulfill their missions, they do not fulfill their destiny, that of educating or entertaining.

The warrior arrives at a large trunk, he opens it: Look at mom, this friction car! I wonder if it still works!

Raising the spring of the mechanism, he launches it. The car crosses the attic from one side to the other and arrives on the opposite wall. On impact, it bounces back, but the friction tries to throw it back on the same wall again.

The Warrior of Light is dreamily observing this cycle: forward - stop - backward - forward - stop - backward...

Some men, like this car or the automatons of yesteryear, do not know how to change direction and are condemned to always reproduce the same cycle: forward - stop - backward - forward - stop - backward...

The Warrior of Light knows that when the lesson is not learned and understood, life represents it to him a second time, then a third and as many times as necessary, to take him to the next level.

But it is not the same in real life as it is for the automaton. If for the automaton the shocks are less and less violent, as he stumbles again, in real life it is quite the opposite! The violence of the shock increases and the price to be paid increases!

The warrior does not want to stumble over the stages of life like the automatons of old, he wants to move forward.

He doesn't want to repeat the same mistakes, that's why he analyzes his days before going to bed.

Thus, he does not take yesterday's mistakes with him the next day; tomorrow will not be like today.

36) The warrior has reached his dream or you have to dream big!

The Warrior has achieved his dream. He reached it in five years instead of ten. Five years of effort rewarded. He rejoices for three days.

On the fourth day, when he wakes up, an angel is at his door, he carries a missive:

- The dream was too small!

37) Perseverance builds great things

or how to introduce small positive routines into one's daily life that will eventually make a big difference without effort.

The Warrior of Light knows that the world is a source of inspiration and wisdom from which he can draw.

He often stays under a large tree where birds are singing. He has long contemplated the perseverance of the mother who, strand after strand, has built his nest.

He has also seen the peasant carrying stone after stone to build his little house in the mountains with his goats.

At the very bottom of the valley, he saw the cathedral of the region and guessed its innumerable stones ...

Perseverance builds great things! he says to himself. [4]

---

[4] Explanations and comments in the second part of the book...

38) Necklaces, bracelets and virtues or for everyone to do what they love or what they excel at.

Today, the Warrior of Light has crossed the vast Pacific Ocean.

He arrived on an island where he was told the inhabitants lived in peace and harmony. There, no one commanded and everyone seemed to obey; it was like a mystery.

What had to be done was done by everyone, without waiting for someone else to order it, so that everyone was in charge and at the same time no one was in charge. The Warrior wanted to know the secret of such a concord.

As soon as the coasts of the island were in sight, the order, beauty and peace that emanated from the shore struck him. He took down his sword from the ship, but he felt that here it would be of no use to him in battle.

One thing intrigues the warrior: everyone wears a necklace of pearls around his neck and sometimes various representations in bracelets on his wrist. Some have one, others two or three, rarely more. But none has his necklace full, nor any of his necklace empty.

The Warrior of Light stops the first man who passes by.

- Hello to you! What's that necklace you're wearing? Does it symbolize something?

- Yes. It is our skill necklace. These pearls are the visible sign of qualities and virtues invisible at first glance: the ability to darn a cloth, to pick commies, to catch fish, or even gentleness, strength, patience, intelligence, courage... the list is almost endless.

- What's the point? asked the Warrior.

- He who excels in one field indicates what that field is and he puts his talent at the service of the other. Conversely, the other puts his service to him in all fairness in the field where he is not so good.

- And how is this necklace built? Who chooses the domains? Who hands it over? I want to know more.

- The necklace is dynamic. Like life, it evolves over time. Each one estimates his own value and chooses the domain where he wishes to blossom.

Sometimes, a resident gives his opinion. He encourages the other to add a skill or to choose another more adapted to his natural abilities. But it is always the person wearing the necklace who decides which beads he adds or removes and the symbols worn on his wrist.

- Why don't children wear a necklace?

- Because until the age of twelve, they look for their motherly virtues and skills. Before and after, they try a multitude of activities.

On their twelfth birthday, their mother and father agree with him and give him his first necklace and bracelet. But as I told you, this necklace is dynamic. It moves like the sky above you and like the sea in front of you.

- So everyone does what they like and what they know how to do best, concludes the Warrior.

- You catch it!

- What if I wanted to wear the pearl of fishing when I haven't practiced it yet?

- It's unusual, but you can wear this pearl if you want. You don't have to be perfect to wear the pearl, you'll take it smaller and make it bigger with your progress, virtue comes with action.

The Warrior marvelled: how these inhabitants had found a simple solution to living together! The Warrior spent some time on this beautiful island and it still remains in his heart.

39) how important the word is

The Warrior knows the value of the word on Earth, as in Heaven. It is by a word that two beings are linked for life on Earth.

It is by a word that the world was founded from Heaven.

A promise is a chain that you put around your neck. He who speaks exposes himself much. He can reveal secrets, speak evil, betray his promises...

This is why the Warrior speaks little. He knows what he commits himself to when he speaks. When a warrior says yes, it is like an oath that commits him, that is why he does not often say yes.

He prefers to remain silent and to carry out... his acts will take care to speak in his place.

40) The Warrior organizes a party to celebrate his victories

The Warrior of Light is happy. The goal he had set for himself has been achieved. He organizes a party. Victory is always more pleasant when joy is shared.

He celebrates his victory with those he loves, because every victory must be celebrated.

His friends arrive, all congratulate him, some envy him, that's life. The warrior savors the present moment, the only one that exists objectively.

Life is also a celebration.

41) The Warrior walks with his Angel, but not only

The Warrior of Light never walks alone. His angel is always at his side to guide and advise him.

He also always walks with his inner child. This one has the custody of his youthful dreams.

He lavishes him with the energy, joy and even carefree carelessness that is sometimes necessary when one embarks on great projects.

The warrior still walks with the old sage within him; the one he will see in the mirror if God lends him life.

And finally the warrior of light walks with himself.

It is by walking in this way that he carries within him the present, the past and the future. That is why he is a Warrior of Light.

42) The aircraft carrier

The Warrior of Light also likes to relax with his friends. He knows that social life is a necessary thing and that friendship is nurtured, otherwise like everything else it withers.

They are all gathered around a table and there he is in their midst. One of them wants to tell a joke: do you know the story of the aircraft carrier off the coast of Newfoundland?
- *No* answer his interlocutors.

Then, happy about its upcoming effect, he begins to tell it with large gestures: It's the story of a transcription between a U.S. Navy ship and the Canadian authorities off the coast of Newfoundland; it seems to be true, he adds excitedly.

The U.S. aircraft carrier USS Abraham Lincoln and its entire escort fleet are on a training maneuver off the Canadian coast of Newfoundland. The operator sees the echo of a ship on his radar. He reports it to his commanding officer, who in turn asks the radio operator to clear the ship by 15 degrees west to clear the way.

The radio operator did so and told the Canadian:
- Please divert 15 degrees west to avoid collision with the US. Navy. Over.

The Canadian radio operator responds to him tactically:
- Negative, we're not moving, we were here first. Please divert 15 degrees west to avoid a collision with us. Over.

The radio operator of the American aircraft carrier insists, but the other does not want to hear anything. So he refers it to his captain who takes the microphone.

- This is the captain of the aircraft carrier Abraham-Lincoln of the United States of America: please quickly change your position by 15 degrees west. Over.

But the other one won't give up:
- We were here first, we will not move a degree: It is up to you to change your course.

Then the commander of the carrier sees red and becomes threatening:

- Let me be very clear with you: This is the aircraft carrier USS Lincoln, the second largest ship in the United States naval fleet. We are accompanied by a significant number of escort ships, including three destroyers, four cruisers and a submarine.

I am ordering you to immediately deviate your course by 15 degrees west, or we will be forced to take coercive action against you, to ensure our safety.

We have at our disposal a firepower so colossal that you cannot even imagine in your worst nightmares the deluge of fire that is likely to descend upon you.

So the Canadian replies:
- Roger that, Captain. This is a lighthouse!

And here is everyone laughing heartily and so is the Warrior.

But now he hears the voice of his Angel who says to him: do you understand the metaphor?

The Warrior is intrigued. The Angel continues:

Man crosses the waves of life armed with his power and draped in his sufficiency.

In the high esteem he has for himself, he thinks in his madness that everything is subject to him. He wants to go straight ahead without considering any obstacle, any difficulty, any prohibition.

And behold, God stands before him immutable, indomitable, who lights the way... What will man do? ...

And the warrior pondered over it.

43) The Warrior refuses to fight!

The Warrior of Light meets many fighters who want to challenge him.

- *Why would I draw my sword*, asks the warrior?

- *We'll see which of us is stronger*, answers the one who challenged him.

- *You are too strong for me*, concedes the warrior who does not want to spill his opponent's blood, just to prove his strength.

By this answer alone, the warrior has avoided many misfortunes.

But sometimes the opponent becomes stubborn and the fight becomes inevitable. Then the warrior draws his sword and acts swiftly. With great determination he engages in the fight that is wrenched from him.

His objective is to draw his sword as quickly as possible, before the other has even laid his hand on the pommel. He wounds his hand so that he does not grab his sword.

The Warrior of Light thus shows his mercy. By wounding the other one in the hand or leg, he prevents him from fighting and saves him from serious injuries and sometimes even saves his life.

Sometimes the warrior is unable to spare his opponent and irreparable damage occurs. The warrior mourns for a long time the one who could have been his friend, but preferred to be his enemy.

By getting to know each other, they would have overcome rivalry and division. They would have found together that many things unite them, more than they would have imagined at first glance.

What would have united them then would have been much stronger than what seemed to divide them.

Yes, the warrior mourns very much for the friend he has lost.

44) The crumb of bread

A man is typing on his computer with a sandwich in his hand. The warrior of light discreetly observes him a few meters away.

A crumb falls on the keyboard. He wants to remove it, but the piece breaks and sinks even deeper. The man gets angry. The more he tries to remove the crumbs, the more they break up and sink.

The warrior approaches the man, greets him and blows hard on the keyboard. All the crumbs fly away. The astonished man watches the warrior walk away with his sword at his side.

There are situations where force is useless. Softness is the best way...

45) The escort of the princess or the force that comes to the aid of the one who loves the good

The king wants to bring his daughter to his wedding, but he has no confidence in the chief of his guard or in the neighboring territory they must cross. He calls for help from the Warrior of Light, an old friend.

- Sends a letter to the future father-in-law and asks for a strong escort, advises the Warrior. If you cannot go to the mountain, let the mountain come to you.

The king follows the advice, but the messenger is intercepted and the letter of reply is changed.

On it is written: *I cannot come to you, lest I create an incident by crossing the neighboring territory. Pass quietly and I will send a guard to my border near the river on such and such a day at such and such a time.*

- This letter seems strange to me, said the Warrior to the king. Have you agreed on a code of trust or a certification? asks the Warrior.

- *No*, answered the king, *I had not thought of that*. The seal is not enough!

- *Some seals are easy to forge*, answers the Warrior.

The journey is decided all the same. The Warrior of Light advises the king: Do not tell the chief of your guard until the last moment.

He remembers that Christ had not told the disciples anything about his last meal, but had secretly sent Peter and John to prepare it. He had done this so that Judas would not have much time to betray him: that is why the warrior had said to the king, "Do not tell the captain of your guard until the last moment".

The great day has come. At dawn, the Warrior woke up the Chief of the Guard and said to him: we are leaving, I am going to choose about ten men, come!

The choice is made and the princess is ready. The procession leaves the courtyard of the palace with muffled footsteps. Here they go. The discreet carriage is escorted by fifteen men and the Warrior of Light.

An hour hasn't gone by that the warrior senses that something is wrong. Several men look at each other, far too often, instead of looking around.

The warrior often changes places in the procession. Sometimes he is in the front, other times in the back, sometimes still on the right or on the left.

- *Why do you move around so much?* the chief of the guard asks worriedly.
- *To ensure the safety of the princess*, answers the warrior.

Yes, and more fundamentally, he tries to evaluate how many guards are in collusion, depending on how they look at her sudden movements. You look at your friends, but you observe and spy on your enemies and the look is not the same.

The report is not good, only two seem to be loyal to the princess. The warrior takes the risk and entrusts his fears to the two men.

He discreetly explains to her the plan they will soon follow, if the others do not attack them beforehand by surprise, and asks them to prepare themselves. They are surprised, but still trust the warrior.

As the three men feared, the other guards turn against them and want to get their hands on the princess.

The Warrior of Light shows by his power, strength and agility why he is called a warrior. He shows no mercy, he cannot afford this luxury, his life and that of the daughter of the king's friend.

His opponents did not expect such heroic resistance that ruins their plan. Taking advantage of their hesitation and the confusion offered by his knightly combativeness, the warrior rushes, intrepidly, towards the princess, tears her from her seat and throws her across his horse. He rides off with his bridle down, shouting at his companions in misfortune to follow him. There are still eight opponents left, they are on their heels, the others are dead. Here they are, taking out their bows and bandaging them.

The warrior cannot at the same time hold the princess, who may fall at any moment, guide her mount, and take out her shield in her back.

He must make a decision if he wants to save her life and the one he is protecting. Then pulling brutally on the side bridle, he forces his horse to jump into the void and falls into the river about fifteen meters below. His companions do the same.

The princess unfortunately cannot swim, she clings to the horse as she can and shakes her legs so as not to sink. Sometimes it is necessary to jump into the water before knowing how to swim.

The warrior pulls out his shield to protect them from the rain of arrows coming down in their direction. The acacia wood shield makes the arrows explode on impact, it is invulnerable to the enemy's arrows; life is as much about defense as it is about attack, the shield as it is about the sword.

The river carries them away. A new volley of arrows, less nourished and less vigorous, comes towards them, as an admission of the powerlessness of the assailants.

Then a striking spectacle is offered to the eyes of those who the moment before seemed lost: the men who were chasing them fall one after the other from their horses, as if they had been hit.

46) The warrior prepares each battle, but not only

The Warrior of Light carefully prepares each battle, when he can foresee them, because he knows that preparation is as important as action.

Many wars have been won or lost even before the first action.

He studies the enemy's strengths and weaknesses and knows his own as well.

The warrior also studies the environment where the battle will take place. A tall warrior is bothered by narrow places, a heavier warrior by soft ground such as mud or sand, others still cannot swim, climb or climb trees. Everyone has his favorite place.

The Warrior attacks in a place which is favorable to him, because he knows that each detail can cost him his life.

47) The warrior shares his meal

The Warrior of Light eats as he prays, with recollection. He appreciates the grace he receives from being able to satisfy his hunger.

Sometimes he shares with those around him when he feels impelled to do so. Today he is content with an orange.

Passers-by to whom he hands a few slices say: *Who is he? What does he want from me? What is he going to ask for in exchange for this food? Is he crazy?*

Isn't it rather this world that is crazy?

And many pass by ignoring this gesture of kindness from the warrior.

But to all those who have accepted it, the warrior has slipped with these accepted slices a prayer of blessing. And those without knowing it also received great blessings from heaven in addition to having tasted the simple happiness of brotherhood.

The most clairvoyant realize this and seek to find the Warrior, but he is nowhere to be found.

The Warrior is unpredictable, he lets himself be guided by the breath and rarely returns to the same places.

Those who want to get in touch with him must look for him in their hearts, because by giving them his own food, he has also given them a little of his soul.

That is where they will find him, in the depths of their hearts.

48) A single blow is not effective

The Warrior of Light observes the fighters to learn from them, especially when the fight is real or when the two opponents are of almost equal levels.

He notes that a single shot is rarely effective at this level of expertise, but a succession of three or more shots often overwhelms the opponent, sometimes even the most accomplished Warrior.

For this reason, the Warrior never allows himself to be hit more than three times in a row without delivering a stop blow to those attacking him.

It is not because the Warrior forgives that he must accept everything; he must remain faithful to his values.

49) The problem is an invitation

The Warrior of Light often smiles when faced with a problem or difficulty.

- *How strange!* say those around him.

The warrior understands that life offers him a training or a challenge depending on the stakes or the complexity of the action.

This challenge will be an opportunity for the warrior to exercise his strength, his intelligence or his tenacity.

Sometimes the warrior cannot solve the problem alone. He understands that this problem was an invitation, not to increase his knowledge, but to increase his relationships with others. Then he goes in search of the one who can help him.

The warrior appreciates the process as much as the result. He trusts life and the star that protects him. He knows that on his way to this problem he will find a friend.

50) The Warrior, His Beauty and Wisdom

The Warrior of Light has heard of a wise man who lives in the mountain, he says to his beloved :

- I am going to the mountain to get wisdom from the one who teaches it.

- Go, my love, I will wait for you and I will see when you return if you are wise.

The warrior goes to the one who must help him to acquire wisdom. When he arrives, he sees him cultivating his field.

The warrior is surprised:

- What are you doing, wise man, cultivating the land?

- Everything is balance and harmony, answers the wise man. And he adds: Just as I take care of the flowers that are outside, I also take care of the flowers of my soul!

He who does not have the patience and discipline to cultivate his garden which he sees growing easily will not have either the discipline and patience to cultivate his inner garden which he sees growing only with a lot of attention.

Strange man that this one calls himself the warrior. But he spent about three months with the wise man and returned to his beloved who was waiting for him, the wise man having told him that he had awakened in him the seeds of wisdom that were already there.

When the Warrior returned to his beloved one, he knocked at the door of her house and heard the voice of her sweet and pure one say to her:

- *Who is there?*

- He answered: *I am your beloved, the one who has gone to seek wisdom.*

- And she answered him:

If you really want to seek wisdom, meditate and come back, for you have not yet grasped it.

The warrior was very surprised, but no matter how much he insisted, the door never opened.

He almost gave in to anger, but he resisted by calming his breath; the lessons he had learned helped him and he went off to the woods to reflect.

He listened for a long time to the song of the birds, which reminded him of his beloved's voice, and he wondered:

- How can she say that I have not yet grasped wisdom when we have hardly exchanged a few words?

He still thinks to himself: *she hasn't understood that it was really me, I'm going back to her and I'm going to insist that she open up to me.*

He went back to her and she asked him the same question: *who is it?*

And he gave the same answer to her beauty, multiplied by the same answer: *I am your beloved, the one who has gone to seek wisdom.*

And he told her again about all the wonderful things they had experienced together, but she always gave him the same answer:

- If you really want to seek wisdom, meditate and come back, for you have not yet grasped it.

Then he returned to the one who had taught him many things. After listening carefully to his account, the teacher answered him:

- Wisdom was with you and you came to me. She is right to tell you that you are still missing one thing; but I cannot offer it to you, for if I offer it to you it would lose its value.

The warrior meditated for a long time until the light of truth illuminated the depths of his soul. Once enlightened, he returned to the one his heart loved.

Faithful, she was waiting for him. She asked him for the third time: who is there?

And the warrior who had understood that wisdom consists in embracing all the facets of the truth in love answered her:
- *You are my beloved and I am your beloved,* so the door opened.

The Warrior of Light had understood that there can be no true wisdom without the decentering of oneself!

He who thinks only of himself cannot be wise, nor can he who thinks only of the other; both are necessary.

51) The Warrior orders his strikes

The best Warriors do not give a succession of moves without order. A disordered succession of musical notes does not give a melody!

These fearsome Warriors order them in an overall strategy. They know that just as piled up materials do not make a house, a mountain of random blows will not build their victory.

The Warrior possesses this knowledge. He works on the fluidity of his sequences. He orders his blows, composes and adjusts them, as one combines notes to make a symphony. Each move brings the next one and amplifies its strength. After a certain number of moves, as in chess, the opponent seems to present his back or his throat as an offering. Fighting is an art!

Whenever possible, because he is a Warrior of Light he lets his opponent live. He tries to make the enemy a friend.
There are so many fights to be fought and good fighters are few...

52) The Warrior gives thanks for the duties he has to accomplish.

Many complain about all the things they have to accomplish in their day and it seems like a burden to them.

The Warrior of Light sometimes shares this feeling as well. But he fulfills his duties, even when they seem painful, and that is how he strengthens himself.

And he noted a surprising thing: duty, once done, brings peace.

In the evening, the Warrior gives thanks for all the tasks that have been entrusted to him and that he has succeeded in carrying out. He is useful in this world.

Strength has been given to him for this day as well. He prays that tomorrow it will be the same.

53) Strength and weakness

The Warrior travels to the two neighboring villages of the Zulu chiefs Uthando (Love) and Ukuthula (Peace) that he has not seen for a long time.

He takes a small path in the savannah and soon notices a strange phenomenon: flowers grow only on one side of the road!

The Warrior continues his way and crosses women of the village, they go to look for water at the well. Then the Warrior proposes to help them, the women refuse:

- It is not a man's work.

The Warrior does not listen to this kind of answer, he knows that everyone needs help and support.

He offers his help again, the women hesitate. One of them hands him the buckets she was carrying. The warrior is happy to be useful and that his strength is useful for something, even in times of peace.

While walking, the warrior notices that one of the buckets is cracked. He lets water ooze along the way, that's why flowers have grown.

The warrior understands that while strength is important, our weaknesses can also be a source of blessings for others.

54) Living life intensely at the risk of being hurt

The small group arrives soon in the village. Uthando approaches with Ukuthula, the three men fall into each other's arms.

The Warrior of Light lets a tear of joy and intense emotion flow.

In the past, he would not have done so. He would not have allowed himself what he considered to be a form of weakness. He would have restrained himself. He had at that time unconsciously decided not to let himself be affected by life and its ups and downs.

He had formed an emotional armor and lived the events of his life, as if at a distance or numb. This made it less painful to face painful events.

But little by little, in order not to be hurt anymore, he had lost his ability to rejoice and love; in a word, to live intensely.

The Warrior had therefore decided to live his life with intensity. He is now out of his waking sleep, he is fully alive.

This is why every day he takes the risk of being hurt, to savor also the risk of being in the flow of life.

He sheds tears of sadness on days of mourning and tears of joy on days of celebration.

55) Everything is linked - Love, peace and light unite their strength

The three men Uthando (Love), Ukuthula (Peace) and the Warrior of Light retreat under the shade of a huge and majestic tree.

The Chiefs want to know how the world is going. They know that what happens in one part of the world affects others; everything is connected.

The news is not good. But more and more Warriors are awakening to consciousness.

The three men pray intensely together for the light to shine as long as possible in the face of the darkness and repel it.

56) The Warrior refuses to die without delivering his melody

The Warrior of Light knows that all men die one day, but many cease to live very young; they have lost the sense of the marvelous, they no longer believe in their dream. They have buried it somewhere in the land of oblivion.

But by burying their dream, they buried with it a bit of their soul and what made them happy. This joy is missing in the world.

He is nostalgic for this painting he will not see, for this music he will not hear, for this music he will not listen to.

The warrior refuses to die without discovering his talents and offering them to men. He does not want to leave without delivering his melody and leave the world what he owes it, the authentic work that he was destined to bequeath to it. It is his choice, it is his destiny; he will fulfill it.

He will give himself to this work until his last breath, until the ultimate limit of his strength; he is a Warrior of Light.

57) There's no need to tear up the painting.

The Warrior of Light knows the power of words. That is why he treats himself with kindness and respect, just as he does with others. The love of others is born in our Heart. If the source is corrupted, no clear water can come out of it to water the world.

It is therefore because he knows the power of words that the Warrior does not say to himself when he has made a mistake:

- *How foolish and stupid you are!* But rather: *I will think about it next time, or here is an idea that is better than the first one.*

His friends who know his philosophy say in a low voice:

- *He's too easygoing with himself! He will never progress!*

The results testify in his favor; they are wrong! The Warrior progresses by successive touches, he improves the picture.

He does not need to tear it up each time!

58) There remains the sin of gluttony

The Warrior of Light works on himself.

He fought one after the other all the dragons that lived in him and that sometimes he even nourished with his thoughts, his words, his actions or more subtly with his omissions: greed, jealousy, anger, fear ... Even the most dangerous one, because it was able to come back to life more easily than the others, the one of pride, was overthrown.

Only one resists that does not seem to him very bad: gluttony. The warrior goes to his mentor and says to him:

- I have conquered fear, shame, envy, anger, judgment, I am free... Gluttony is still there, but it is not much... eight of the nine deadly sins, isn't that excellent?

The mentor remains silent.

- Follow me, he simply says

He takes her to the port, and here is a large sailboat attached to the quay. He cast off and is about to leave with all sails out. Then the master puts the rope back to the mooring cock that the man on the quay had untied.

The boat is trapped. It is pitching, cracking, and breaking apart. He tries to free himself, but comes back to himself. The sailors on board panic and do not understand what is happening.

One of them soon notices the rope attached and the two men beside it. The master does not pay attention to him. Taking advantage of the boat that has come back within his reach, he attaches a second rope.

- *What are you doing!* said the warrior to him, *they are going to crash!*

- The sailor shouts: *what are you doing there! Our sails are out, we have to leave. Please free us, otherwise we will perish!*

The master frees the two moorings that were holding the ship, the ship is finally free and is leaving.
- *Have you understood?*

Yes, the Warrior has understood. He will never reach the promised port if he remains attached to one of his sins. He will soon call a second one, then a third one, and finally all will catch up with him; soon he will die miserably.

Then in joy, the Warrior goes back to work. For every meal he has a piece of bread and clear water in a wooden bowl. Tonight he will take vegetables; that makes him happy.

59) The Warrior proposes the path or choose to cross the world with a pure and light heart.

The Warrior of Light does not judge anyone, not even himself. He observes cause and effect.

He simply evaluates what brings him closer to his goals and what takes him away from them. He also listens to his heart and acts in accordance with his values; he is true to himself.

Sometimes he proposes a path to others and enlightens them by his example. Virtues are worthwhile only by their application.

Those who receive the invitation are free to accept or refuse it. Some do and some do not.

Judgment and hatred have no place in the heart of the Warrior of Light. Nor does he carry them on his back, for they are heavy to bear, as is sadness. It is not for the Warrior to carry them.

Thus, he does not condemn those who have turned their backs on him. They are free. It is from their freedom that their merit comes.

The Warrior has chosen to cross the world with a pure and light heart, and everything is simpler.

However, the Warrior thinks of them, especially when evening falls: what becomes of them?

Sometimes a star appearing in the sky gives him the answer.

Other times the wind whispers a confidence in his ear and reveals the secret.

Sometimes his question remains unanswered, that is the mystery, God keeps his secret.

60) The warrior laughs heartily or keeps a child's heart

The Warrior of Light laughs heartily at a funny story.

- *How ingenuous he is*, exclaims his friends!

The Warrior of Light knows that laughter is very good for health. Only those with a childlike soul know how to appreciate certain things.

He remembers that Christ said:
"Blessed are those who have the soul of a child, for theirs is the kingdom of heaven. "

Then the Warrior laughs and lets them laugh at his expense. He knows that this laughter is actually praise.

They too would like to have a child's soul, but they can no longer find the way to their heart.

61) One day he will pass to the other side of the mirror.

The Warrior of Light knows that everything goes its way, nothing is immutable; not even mountains.

He himself had been lucky enough to see a mountain collapse in an instant under the onslaught of rain, while he was sheltering on the nearby mountain.

He also saw a whole section of cliff collapse under the crash of the waves as he walked along one of them.

One day it will be his turn to go to the other side of the mirror.

But he is at peace. He knows that an even better world awaits him, a world of light and joy, that's what the warriors who entered the tunnel of light and came back told him.

Some people don't believe it. Yet there are so many messengers carrying the same message of hope that one can only be certain of the message. There are far too many of them for this to be an illusion.

The original beauty of this world, the gratuitousness and abundance of the goods that were there in the beginning certify it, they say it is true: love and joy await us.

Death is not an end, but a passage to something greater and better.

The Warrior is at peace.

62) Stroll by the sea or how one can change history

The Warrior of Light is walking by the sea. At the bend of a large cove, he sees fishermen. They are deploying all their strength to bring a net back to the beach. The net is overflowing with fish. With each movement of the waves, they pull in unison:

- O Heave! ... O Heave! ... O Heave ! ...

The fish are frightened, they feel their last hour approaching. They struggle, pulling each one in its own direction. It is panic, the net tightens. They are disorganized, unlike the men who lead them where they would not want to go. Some, in their terror, even swim ashore without knowing it.

The warrior soon notices a fish in the net that behaves differently. It is much stronger than the others and seems to know exactly what it is doing. He swims resolutely towards the open sea and makes his power known to the men. He resolutely refuses to succumb to them.

He alone puts the fishermen in difficulty for a while, but the fish is hindered in its struggle by the others who go in all directions. The men organize themselves. They call for reinforcements; they will soon be there.

Before they arrive, several fish become one with the valiant fish. They unite their strength and break the stitches. It was about time! The reinforcements are there, now the net is in the hands of the men. The fishes that remained trapped are now at their mercy.

The men celebrate their victory. As for those who escaped, they have retreated far from the shore. The warrior guesses the shoal in the distance with the wriggling of the surface. They are celebrating freedom and life; in a way they too are celebrating their victory!

The warrior wonders how many were able to save themselves. An angel blows him their number: they are 153. Walking along the shore, he remembers the scene, everything started with the brave fish, but alone he would not have survived.

The Warrior of Light understands that he will not be able to defeat alone…

63) Not everything is accomplished

It's good to step back, to look behind you.

The magnificent work in which the warrior participates is not only beyond his efforts, it is also beyond his consciousness.

During his life, he will realize only a small part of the magnificent enterprise that is God's work.

The Warrior has not been given the mission to do everything, much less to do everything alone. Nothing he does is completed or so little! The Kingdom of love, peace and joy that he wants to see is always beyond his possibilities.

No statement says all that he would like to say. No prayer completely expresses the depths of his heart. No religion brings the fullness of God. No struggle brings total victory over evil.

The warrior of light plants seeds that he may never see growing, but that will not stop him from sowing. One day they will grow, if God so wills; they carry within them the promise of the future.

The warrior sometimes lays the foundation on which others will build. He sometimes adds a floor to the existing building or straightens up the one that was leaning excessively and threatened to fall.

It is this leaven that makes a whole dough rise. It will produce effects multiplied far beyond its human capacities alone.

This understanding brings him a sense of liberation and allows him to do something even imperfectly rather than doing nothing at all. The work is not finished, but it is already a beginning. Another warrior will come who will finish it or make it grow.

The Warrior has fulfilled his destiny; he has fulfilled himself by developing the talents that have been deposited in him, and he has offered them to the world.

He has placed his stone on the great path of life.

Help for symbolic understanding of the stories.
Comments - Possible implications in life.

64) Fighting with the master or how to become a master after being a disciple

What is a master? What is the relationship with the disciple?

The master is the one who has the knowledge and ability to lead. He is at the same time a model to be imitated, a teacher and a guide. He naturally inspires respect, admiration and sometimes even veneration or love in those who follow him.

Because of his supremacy in many areas, he possesses a certain power over others. This power is also intrinsic to the master-disciple relationship, because in a certain way the disciple has renounced his own power in favor of the one who leads him.

This director can consequently exercise a certain power. This can awaken in the disciple a feeling of fear born of the conviction that he is at the mercy of the one who also serves as his model.

There is a second field of paradox. The master, although he is the model to be imitated, who is very close, also symbolizes an ideal to be reached which seems inaccessible, a horizon.

But what is beyond this horizon? The disciple might ask himself this question. He could ask himself another very concrete one: what would happen if several masters were to confront each other?

The answer is obvious: many would lose. No matter how strong a master may be, he is not invulnerable.

The master-disciple relationship is therefore ambivalent. To all the positive dispositions, attitudes and feelings such as :
respect, trust, veneration, love ... sometimes oppose: fear, suspicion, mistrust.
All these ambivalences arise in history when the disciple fears to face his master, when normally he should have confidence in him.
The fact that the Warrior of Light accepts to obey him, even if reluctantly, shows that he is still under the domination of his master at this moment in history.

The master of the warrior is a good master. He does not want his disciple to remain perpetually under his control, but on the contrary, he wants him to go through the process of learning and transformation. To do so, he must cross the ultimate obstacle of his path of liberation. This "final" obstacle on the path of the disciple ... is the master himself!

The one who had to be imitated in the past, must now be overcome!

This story is therefore an invitation to surpass oneself.

The two essential characteristics to become a master.

The outcome of the fight is uncertain, because one is never certain to overcome one's fears.

From the point of view of history, this indecision in the victory of one or the other is the proof that both fighters are almost at the same level.

The disciple puts the master in difficulty and thinks he has him in his power. The disciple has thus progressed a lot since the first day. He is no longer the one he used to be. An inversion of hierarchy appears here.

But the master brings out another weapon more adapted to close combat. Two reflections on this point of the story.

First, a master is a person who has resourcefulness. He is able to cope, even when the situation seems desperate; and it is this state of mind and level of expertise that one must aim for, if one wants to become a master.

Second, the disciple is still naive. Certainly, he has the technical mastery, but that is not enough. He must also get to know people. This lack of knowledge could have cost him his life. There is a lesson here for leaders.

Even if they keep their lives, they can still waste a lot of time, energy and money by not knowing who they are working with, just thinking that one man is worth another.

No! there is always one who is better suited for a given task or mission.

Fortunately, the Warrior of Light changes his mind, changes tactics and wins.

At the end of the story, it is the one who was once his master who implores him. The hierarchy is reversed.

By his final declaration: You have won, the former master acknowledges the victory of the one who was once his disciple. He also recognizes his new authority, leaving him the pre-eminence of choice: Let me teach where you will not be!

Be capable of greatness of soul.

Finally, the phrase: Choose life and spare me is the last teaching of a master to his disciple, like his will. It is an invitation to become aware that there is a choice to be made here: life or death.

The warrior is not obliged to kill his opponent. The former master (who is still a master at heart, although no longer the warrior) gives here a final lesson to his disciple. The rest of the book shows that he will be faithful to it.

The respect of the Warrior of Light for the one who formed him and his greatness of soul can be seen in the life he keeps for him, but not only.

It is easier to stay in place when you are wounded, when you have your house, your garden, your life ... than to leave. By yielding all this to the one who formed him, the Warrior of Light objectively favors his master. And he also shows his rectitude.

He accomplishes justice. Victory does not authorize everything, especially the injustice of taking everything from the one who has lost or is weaker.

By leaving, the warrior recognizes the authority of his defeated opponent on this place: Here is your domain, but more on his soul, which is manifested by his departure.

To be free and to realize oneself.

Finally, this departure is symbolic of liberation.

Every man is invited to overcome his fears if he wants to be truly free and realize himself. Man's great fears are obstacles that govern, direct and control his life.

I am not talking here about phobias like that of spiders or that of flying, but about man's fundamental fears: to be controlled by others, to be rejected or hurt, the fear of lack of resources, to be judged, the fear of suffering, the fear of failure ...

Man (represented here by the Warrior of Light), will only be perfectly free (manifested by his departure, at the end of history) if he faces his fears.

The Warrior of Light must face what he fears the most, if he wants to evolve at his best and reach his full realization.

According to his history, man is more or less fragile towards one (or several) of these fears. The disciple who has become aware of these fears is already advanced on the path to liberation and can choose to face them.

Conversely, if he is unconscious of them, the road ahead will be longer. For how can one fight and defeat an adversary whom one does not know and who one does not see! In this case, one must first go in search of one's fears.

This process requires external help or, better still, self-observation in order for them to reveal themselves.

This self-observation is not a judgment, but a detached observation of our non-adapted behaviors; then we can remedy it.

This will not happen overnight, but with gentle and firm perseverance, we will get there.

This stage of discovering one's fears and confronting them is essential for the full realization of the potential dormant in each man and I say even for the blossoming of his true personality.

Such is, for example, the allegory of the dragon guarding the treasure. All these riches and their benefits will only be ours when we have confronted the dragon and defeated it.

After this hard and often painful fight, an era of abundance, peace and joy opens up for the one who has defeated.

65) The fire lit by the children or how to carry out any project with enthusiasm, measure and perseverance

Fire is the image of desire. It is not only sexual desire, but all things or states that one is deeply motivated to attain.

There is a state of excitement at the beginning of the project. This is manifested by the joy of the children.

Man, unconscious of all the work that will be done, throws himself into it, going in all directions; this is what the children do by putting in the fire just about everything that passes under their hands.

In this period of enthusiasm, he is very active. He reads a lot of things, documents himself, eventually talks about it around him, tries to practice ... The project has just started, it's time for joy!

But man has an impatient nature. He would like to arrive before he leaves, to have an athletic body before doing sports, to lose weight before starting food hygiene, to have new knowledge before studying, to be calm before meditating...

Attracted by his desire to reach his goal as quickly as possible, he neglects the process that leads to it, he wants to suppress it. He does not understand that it is precisely this process time that will make the future transformation more stable.

So, burning the steps, he wants to do too much; this is what happens when the big log is added. Instead of doing the 5 or 10 minutes of meditation that would have sufficed at the beginning, we aim for one hour, we hold on for a few days. Then not having the strength to support this new constraint that we imposed on ourselves, we bend under the load, the pleasure is no longer there!

Little by little, it changed into a constraint then into a burden to carry.

Disillusioned, we abandon the load and the project dies. It leaves in our mind the ashes of the dream we had some time earlier.

It would have been better to gradually increase our demands on ourselves and we would have had the training to support this higher level of practice.

This story is therefore an invitation to patience and to the kaizen method of small steps: it is better to make the fire grow first.

66) Perseverance builds great things or how to introduce small positive routines into one's daily life that will make a big difference in the long run, without effort

Man loves great feats of brilliance, dazzling victories. He underestimates the power of repeated efforts and the cumulative benefit they bring.

Four unfortunate minutes a day repeated over a year gives a whole day at the end of the year; that's three big eight-hour days.

For getting my children to wait for their bus, with a book in hand, rather than getting lost in their phones or aimlessly staring at passers-by, I got them not only to read a lot of books, but better yet, to love reading.

Anyone who spends only ten minutes a day looking at their messages on their phone or otherwise has already seen sixty hours of their life evaporate in a year.

Thus, in the cumulative vision, ten minutes is worth sixty hours!

The amplification effect that comes from the power of repetition works both ways: to our benefit or to our detriment.

In history, perseverance builds great things, it is always in the right direction that things evolve (this book is meant to be an optimistic and encouraging book).

There are, however, two different scales. The mother bird and the peasant on the one hand and the builders of cathedrals on the other.

The mother bird is no less noble than the peasant in her construction, even if her nest is more fragile.

She builds a house to her measure, and her efforts to carry the strands and all the building materials are no less admirable than that of the peasant. Each one of them carries what he is capable of carrying.

If the first two will certainly see the end of their work, the same cannot be said of those who participated in the beginnings of the sumptuous religious construction.

Another major difference is the collaboration needed to build the cathedral, which does not appear in that of the nest or even the house.

To build very great things, one must not be alone and this is what the warrior fully understands at the end of the book with the story of the fish.

67) The disciple and the reflection on the lake or how to find inspiration

This story begins in the evening. The young man did not want his visit to be known by the other villagers. This nocturnal visit shows the discretion that the young man wants to cover his visit.

From a spiritual point of view, this means that the search for wisdom should not be done with ostentation, but with discretion, as in the night. It is only after this time of introspection that the light we have received in the shadow of recollection will spring forth as pearls of light.

For now, we must dive into the depths of our being.

From a metaphorical point of view, this night is an image of the confusion that reigns in the young man's mind. By visiting the Warrior of Light, he feels that he will be able to help him see more clearly. He will be like a star pointing to a safe direction and guiding him on his journey.

In fact, it is a good idea to go to a qualified person for advice on how to behave. This is what we do without realizing it when we go to see a doctor when we are sick, or a dentist when we have a toothache, or a lawyer in case of litigation...

The young man indicates the object of his request; it is neither money nor fame, but wisdom (I would like to be as wise as you), which reveals his greatness of soul.

How to recognize a wise man?

A dialogue takes place between the two men. The Warrior of Light asks him: Who said I was wise?

The warrior by asking this question does not answer that he is indeed wise, nor does he say that he is not. He leaves the young man's assertion open.

If he had answered that he was truly wise, it would have been at the very least pretension and at the worst madness.

In either case, he would have proved that he is not the one claimed.

No wise man would claim to be, because he knows his limits. He knows that all wisdom is relative. In an asylum for the insane, a person quite average in the world appears for the insane locked up or supremely wise or completely insane herself.

Wisdom could still be compared to wealth. A person who is a millionaire is rich for common people, but for a billionaire he is a thousand times less rich than he is! Even if both appear rich to the common man, one is much richer than the other!

A wise man challenges by his words and his behavior. He draws a line of division between the two, which provokes antinomic reactions: in the village many say it and others retort that you are crazy.

The line between madness and wisdom or even genius may appear thin to some people, because each of the two is at the end of the spectrum of the human person and, seen from the middle, they are difficult to distinguish from each other.

The Warrior of Light answers him: because some say I am mad, then perhaps I am wise, for wisdom seems mad to those who are stuck in the world.

By his answer, the master indicates that true wisdom is taken for madness, by common people; (this is why true sages are rare, they are out of the norm).

The Warrior of Light thus shows that he is truly wise. His answer impresses the young man, since he says to him: I see that you are a Master of thought. Which the warrior does not contradict.

What is the price to pay?

The disciple, before committing himself fully, inquires about the price to pay: How long will it take me to acquire Wisdom? This is the mark of a far-sighted spirit.

The Warrior of Light answers: It depends on you. Some of the best disciples took two years, others five, others ten, and some went before that.

The disciples who preceded him, though all had the same master, did not all take the same amount of time to reach the goal; worse, some failed!
There is here a proof of the sincerity of the master and his humility, since he even admits "his failures".

The task does not frighten the future disciple. He is ready to work twice as hard as the best of them, to reach his goal more quickly: If I work twice as hard as the best of them will I take a year instead of two?

There is a kind of blindness or pretension here. How do you know if you are capable of accomplishing twice as much as a man you know nothing about! Perhaps he worked - twenty hours a day! Will we be able to work forty hours in a twenty-four hour day?

However, the master is not going to stop on this point, which is, after all, quite obvious.

He will go on to another much more hidden point.

If in a mechanistic vision of things one arrives twice as soon by going twice as fast, it is not the same in the spiritual realm.

It is precisely this haste that is opposed to the quietude that precedes the attainment of wisdom. A restless mind will never be able to contemplate it. This is what the warrior wants to bring him to understand by taking him to the lake.

How to let oneself be inspired?
Or the fruits of a calm soul.

This lake is an image of the disciple's soul. If it is calm, it reflects the sky. One can then see on its surface down to the reflection of the smallest stars and collect their light.

Thus, according to the Warrior of Light, wisdom comes from the sky. It is "enough" to put oneself in a state of receptivity to receive it from above. The soul must be like a white canvas waiting for the Virtuoso Painter to come and place his work on it.

This state of receptivity is only possible in calm and quietness. Wisdom is not knowledge, although it weaves intimate ties with it.

One can be very erudite, but not possess it, and conversely, know very little and be truly wise.

It is not something that can be acquired by wrist strength and study.
Wisdom is like the fruit that is grown in a greenhouse. They look like orchard fruit, but they don't taste like it.

They are eaten, but they do not satisfy, they do not fill, while from the fruits of wisdom received from above, a single sentence can fill a whole life!

Bonus

68) The Warrior of Light and the Mathematician

The Warrior of Light decides to increase his logic because it is one of the forms of intelligence and he needs it for his survival.

He goes to see an old sage who was once also an illustrious mathematics teacher. He questions him:

- *How can I increase my logic?*
- *Like anything else, by exercising it*, the wise man answers him.
- *Can you give me an example that I can understand better?*

The Wise One knows that theory is nothing without practice and application. He presents him with this problem: A Captain of the China Sea has 25 goats and 15 buffaloes on his boat... How old do you think he is?

The Warrior of Light remains perplexed! How to know the age of the captain by knowing the number of animals he carries? It doesn't make any sense !

The warrior thinks that maybe there is a trick, that if he simply adds up the numbers it might give him the right result:

- *I would say he is 40 years old. This seems a rather plausible number to me and it is the sum of the number of animals.*

- *And if he loses a goat along the way, will he be a year younger*, the mathematician says mischievously.

- *How do you expect me to know how old he is!* finally answered the warrior, somewhat annoyed, wondering if he is not wasting his time. I don't know. I don't have enough information.

- *Very well*, said the wise man, *then I'll give you two more: the goats are three years old on average and the buffaloes eight.*

- *It doesn't help me to know that either!* replied the Warrior.

- *But you told me that you didn't have enough information. I'm giving you more, and you're not happy.*

- *It's not what I need!*

- *At least you learned one thing today. It's not the quantity of information that will help you solve your problems, but the quality of it. Come back to see me tomorrow and we'll talk.*

The next day, after much hesitation, the warrior goes back up the mountain. This story intrigues him and he wants to get to the bottom of it. The old man says that the problem has a solution, yet he sees none. The Warrior nevertheless feels that the key that the wise man will give him will open his mind.

- *Hello to you*, the Warrior says to the man sitting on his stone.

In front of his hut, he contemplates high in the sky three great eagles that turn tirelessly like the hands of a well-oiled clock.

- *The weather will be fine today*, the wise man answers.
- *I see some threatening clouds, however!* retorts the warrior.

- *This species of eagle has its plumage which is not as well oiled as that of wild ducks. They only fly at this height in good weather. That's why I know it will not rain; their flight tells me so.*
- *Very well*, said the warrior, *I will know in the future. Some of my horses don't like rain or mud,*

and they let me know when I take them out in this
weather, while others like it.

The warrior tells himself that life is full of surprises. In trying to solve a problem, one sometimes solves a second one that is at least as important as the first, if not more so.

Coming out of his thoughts, the Warrior throws to the wise: *Let's return to our problem as a captain. Can you tell me his age?*
- *No*, answers the wise man, but I can on the other hand give you a clue and an advice.

There he goes again, the Warrior thinks to himself. Decidedly, this teacher is not like the others. Why don't you just give the answer! he said to the mathematician.

- Curiosity is the spring of learning. If I told you the solution too soon, you would stop thinking for yourself and progressing; I would break the spring of your learning.

The Warrior meditated for a moment on this link between curiosity and learning. Interesting, he thought, I would have to implement this link in my interactions with my disciples.

This man gets different results because he uses different methods. If he used the same methods as everyone else, he would have the same results as everyone else in almost every way.

So he reconsidered the situation and said to himself that what he saw as a waste of time to have stumbled upon this somewhat strange mathematician was certainly a blessing. It is those who are not like us who can bring us the most.

- *I'm listening to you*, he finally answered.
- *Well, the boat is 23 meters long*, declares the wise man with a mischievous look, certain of its small effect.

There he goes again! says the warrior.
- *That's your clue!* Can you give me the advice?
- *Go down to the harbor, maybe you will meet this famous captain!*

He is laughing at me, thinks the warrior...

After a moment's hesitation, he greets the old man with a smile on his face and leaves, actually a little displeased to have wasted his time... at least he thinks so at that moment.

- *Come back to me with the answer*, says the wise man.

- *Nothing is less sure*, answers the warrior, who, if he unfortunately has some faults, at least tries not to lie.

And here is the warrior who comes down from the mountain. Arrived in the valley he hesitates, what should he do: go to the right to go down to the port or return directly to his home?

He finally decides to clear up this story and arrives at the docks. It had been a long time since he had been there. And just now a big boat is maneuvering to enter the port.

The warrior notices the skill of the captain and his crew. In fifteen minutes they tie their moorings to the quay. The sailors are busy getting the cargo down: barrels of alcohol and bags of rice. The captain is on the deck of his ship watching his men work.

The warrior wants to know more about this man. He walks towards the ship and calls out to the captain:

- *I want to go up and talk to you, is that possible, now that the maneuver is over? I will only have a few minutes, it is in order to know how to become a captain.*

The Warrior knows that men are by nature distrustful of their fellow men, especially when they are men of influence.

They quickly want to know who they are dealing with and what they want, that's why the Warrior gave so many explanations about his desire to ascend. Clarifying one's intentions reassures many and also the time it will take.

- Go upstairs, but I can only give you a few minutes, ten at the most, I still have a lot of things to sort out.

The Warrior climbs aboard quickly. Here he is chatting with the captain. And out of the discussion comes the light. The Warrior now knows the captain's age, well, sort of. Happy, he goes back down and puts his steed in the saddle, he whips his mount in the joy of discovery and here he is soon back to the wise man.

- To what do I owe the honor of a second visit on the same day? asks the man with a touch of mischief.

- I wish to discuss with you about the captain's age.

- Come, we will discuss over a cup of tea. I knew you would come back.

- There, I will say that he is about thirty years old!

- Very well, I share your opinion. And how did you arrive at this deduction?

- Well, by talking with the captain, he taught me that to transport animals or anything else on a boat longer than fifteen meters, you need a special permit. This is only issued if the holder is more than 23 years old. Since the captain's boat is twenty, this rules out the possibility that he is less than 23 years old. And since the license is withdrawn after the age of 63, the maximum age of exercise, it is therefore obligatorily between 23 and 63 years old.

- It's true, the wise man tells him. *But without having discussed with this man you could have deduced it: a child cannot drive, nor an old man. This already excludes many possible values for someone with even a simple marine license.*

The Warrior of Light understands his mistake better. If you want to be too exact from the first time, you risk being stuck and doing nothing, because you think you lack information. This can lead to a gradual drift away from the goal and miss out on good opportunities.

- But why exactly 30 years? asks the mathematician.

- Well, the man also told me that the license was rarely issued before 25 years. So it is unlikely that our man is under 25. He said that merchants prefer to trust experienced men. He finally added that it is difficult to have both the money to buy a boat and to find customers who trust newcomers. The well-established captains on their side had the luxury of being able to choose their merchants. And the more time went by, the fewer animals they carried, because it was quite a story. First of all, they would let loose in the ship and it was very painful to wash it all afterwards. This would stop the ship for a few more hours to prepare it to load the next load, especially if it was food.

Also, the animals would sometimes panic, especially when the weather was bad. They would then fight among themselves or even load the crew members. This resulted in many shipwrecks. As a result, only the new captains were still carrying animals.

It usually took 10 years to make a name for oneself in this business. So considering that he had obtained his license at 25 years old at the earliest, and that from the age of 35 he would no longer transport animals, I deduced that his most probable age was around 30 years old.

- *Very well*, said the wise man, *you have reasoned well.*

We don't know how old this captain really is, because we don't have all the information, but just because we don't have all the information doesn't mean we don't know anything! Some things are possible and some things are impossible!

So, by logic, statistics or intuition you will be able to distinguish one from the other. Logic will not always allow you to reach the truth in your heart, but it will at least allow you to get close to it. You will be like a man without his glasses who without seeing perfectly well can still distinguish shapes and can walk in the right direction.

As for your intuition, you have to work on it and nourish it by embracing similar situations or proceeding by analogy, your unconscious brain will give you the answer when you are relaxed.

The warrior asked the wise man a question: *How did you know I would come back?*

- This is a statistical truth. I apply the truths I teach to myself; this is what distinguishes Masters from recitors. So I knew it, because I know the statistical law underlying your behavior.

He who returns three times to the same problem returns a fourth time. This is true 90% of the time... Let's say I knew it 90% of the time... This probability is more than enough to form an opinion!

The Warrior coming down from the mountain meditated on all his words.

He told himself that their scope was extremely vast and that he would take a considerable amount of time to apply the wisdom hidden in what he had experienced; the Captain's age was after all only secondary.

The main thing was elsewhere and in particular in front of him: what would he do with all he had learned?

69) A last word

This book is deeper than it appears at first glance. This is why I invite the reader, with gentle insistence, to reread it several times; not necessarily in succession, although this is not a bad idea, but rather a few days or even weeks apart. His reading will seem changed. He will see new meanings in what he had read before.

It will often be an unveiling that awaits him. It will seem to him that certain passages have been added, by an invisible hand.

Sometimes it will be the other way around. A part, or a message that seemed important to him will be re-revealed and covered by another!

That each time he meditates, and even better, writes down these meditations and reflections, that is how he will benefit the most.

Where does this mystery come from?

Just as the Sun (intelligence) does not always produce the same reflections on the sea (our soul or our life), I have associated words, just as a painter associates colors so that some people see green, when others see blue, or yellow instead of green, or vice versa.

Depending on his position, depending on the lighting (of his soul), he will sometimes lean towards one color and sometimes towards another. Neither is truer or less true than the other. Both are true the instant they are perceived.

Thus, like a painter using an almost infinite palette, the sun does not always shine in the same way and the sea is not always the same, so that the reflections change.

Whether it is gold or silver, whether it is lighter or darker, life flows and the painting changes. Watch it change, appreciate the beauty of this dynamic creation and enjoy the journey...

70) Invitation

The reader who wishes to do so can write to : leguerrier.delaluz@gmail.com

to give his impressions, his thoughts and the feelings that these stories brought out in him.

He can also simply say the five, six, seven, ... ten stories he liked best and why not, the one(s) he didn't like.

He is also invited, if he wishes, to participate in the second opus which is already in preparation, by proposing one or more stories, illustrative drawings or simply a sentence that he would like the warrior to pronounce.

The names of those who proposed the stories, illustrations and sentences selected may appear (or not, depending on their desire) in the book.

Acknowledgements

I thank for its translation Mr. Philippe Elie-Auzée, the original text being in French.

I thank for their observations, improvements, comments, corrections and advices: my mother, Marie-Noëlle AUBRY, my grandmother, Ginette SALINIERE, my children, Ludovic, Anthony and Laurence, my mother-in-law, Lucette LEMAIRE, my aunts, Maryvonne SALINIERE, and Chantal LUCIDE, my cousin, Olivia SABIN.

I would also like to thank all those whom I have not mentioned and who, in great numbers, have made the conception and realization of this book possible through their support, their kindness and their encouragement.

Finally, my thoughts turn to the men who have served as models for me:

My father, Guy AUBRY, my grandfather, Serge SALINIERE, my uncles, especially Frantz SABIN... all warriors of the light....

Table des matières